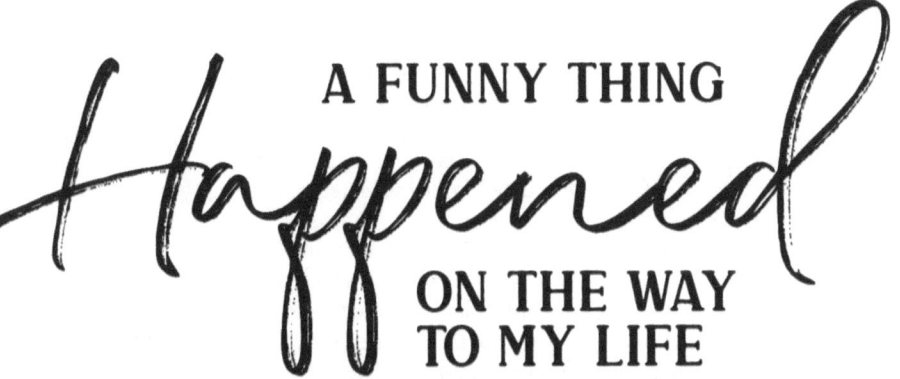

A FUNNY THING Happened ON THE WAY TO MY LIFE

LAURA MUIRHEAD

Copyright © Laura Muirhead
First published in Australia in 2024
by KMD Books
Waikiki, WA 6169

Cover photo © Maria-Ines Fuenmayor

All rights reserved. No part of this book may be used or reproduced by any means, graphic, electronic, or mechanical, including photocopying, recording, taping or by any information storage retrieval system without the written permission of the copyright owner except in the case of brief quotations embodied in critical articles and reviews.

The perspective of events included in this book may be different than the perspective of others.

Because of the dynamic nature of the Internet, any web addresses or links contained in this book may have changed since publication and may no longer be vaild. The views expressed in this work are solely those of the author and do not necessarily reflect the views of the publisher and the publisher hereby disclaims any responsibility for them.

A catalogue record for this work is available from the National Library of Australia

National Library of Australia Catalogue-in-Publication data:
A Funny Thing Happend on the Way to My Life / Laura Muirhead

This is for anyone who has kept their story quiet for far too long.

Thanks to those who have helped me heal and grow.

I am grateful for everyone who has supported and encouraged me to tell my story.

INTRODUCTION

Many people experience a life-changing event at some point in their lives. Maybe it's a house fire, a lottery win, or their parents' divorce. Some go through their own divorces (or two), while others uncover long-buried family secrets, like discovering an unexpected relative. Some find purpose by building a business - a bread store, a horse stable, or an art studio. Some embark on these journeys alongside a partner.

And then there's me. I've experienced all of this and more, which is why I like to say, "A Funny Thing Happened On the Way to My Life®."

I don't allow any one challenge or unplanned plot twist to define me. What I've learned is that resilience is key to navigating life's unpredictable turns. Each unexpected twist comes with its own challenges, but these challenges present opportunities to learn, grow, and evolve. It's not the obstacle itself that matters - it's how we choose to respond. For me, that response is rooted in gratitude. When you can find gratitude in even the most difficult situations, that's when peace settles in. That's when transformation happens.

Throughout my life, I have refused to let conventional or societal norms dictate how I live, react, or evolve. Instead, I've embraced each curveball as a chance to adapt, to grow stronger, and to keep moving forward. Whether it was a financial windfall, the loss of a home, or the discovery of my biological father after 40 years, I chose not to let these moments control my narrative. I saw them as stepping stones that shaped me into who I am today.

I find myself now, in the sixth decade of my life, standing at a place of immense gratitude. I'm grateful not only for the successes but also for the challenges, as they have been my greatest teachers. Today, I'm confident and comfortable in who I am, both personally and professionally. I am a wife, a mother of grown children, and an adopted mama to two lovable Labrador Retrievers. I am also co-owner, vice-president, and CFO of a thriving family business.

But that's only part of my story. I'm also an artist, a healer, and a sage. I've created the Queen Code program and its Oracle Card Deck, tools that have helped women worldwide transform their lives. I've published books, become an international best-selling author, and embraced my role as a LightWeb® Priestess, using universal energy and my intuition to help guide others. My husband and I own homes in two states and enjoy the freedom to travel, explore new adventures, and continue to build a full and balanced life. I make time for my creative passions - whether that's drawing, pottery, photography, or crocheting - while balancing my professional responsibilities.

As you read on, I hope my story reminds you that no single challenge or unexpected plot twist defines you. Life unfolds in ways we can never predict. When a funny thing happens on the way to *your* life - because it will - I encourage you to find strength in resilience, to seek gratitude in the moment, and to trust that each twist in the road brings growth, opportunity, and wisdom.

CHAPTER 1
CHILDHOOD

Imagine your soul standing right on the verge of beginning your earthly mission.

"What is it that you'd like to experience as a human this time?" you're asked.

Taking a moment to think about what you've done in the past, all the experiences you've had over various lifetimes, you respond, "I want the full buffet. Gimme it all. Don't leave anything out. I don't want to be bored."

"Are you sure? I know you've had many opportunities in the past … but so much in one lifetime?"

Confidently you counter, "I'm sure I can handle it. I'll be able to take each lesson in stride. And I want to share my knowledge to help others as well."

"Ok … if you're positive. You'll get the full menu, personal wins and losses, catastrophic weather events, and even a couple of big surprises. It may even feel like multiple lifetimes in one. Of course, you won't remember our conversation, so you won't be prepared or see the twists and turns coming your way."

"Sounds amazing!" your soul answers.

"Ready then? I see the perfect crazy situation for you to be born into."

"Ready!"

"Then off you go…I know you'll do great."

And it's true - I don't remember. But that's what it must have been like because of all the amazing things that have happened.

The story of our lives, the stories we believe are our lives, begin with our family and where we are born. It's usually one of the first things people ask you. Where are you from? Or where do you live? And what about your family? These stories form for us from the beginning. For me, the story of my life began in the midwest, in a suburb of Chicago. I was the youngest of two girls born into a middle-class family. See how quickly there is a story for our lives? Then there is the larger family circle. My earliest years were spent in the town where I was born surrounded by my grandparents, aunts, uncles, and cousins. They all lived either in the same town or the adjacent towns.

My mom's parents had five kids. They were the ones that

lived near us, and I can remember visiting their house, usually to find that my cousins were already there. These were my earliest memories of that side of the family; playing with my cousins and spending time at my grandparents' house. My parents and my aunt and uncle went to the same church. My cousin and I were in the same Sunday school class. Solid family connections. At that age, my life was that small nucleus. Our house, neighborhood, town, and family. I remember going to kindergarten and riding the bus. One day I somehow missed getting off at my stop. So, I got off at the next stop in my neighborhood and started walking … hopefully in the right direction … to my house, tears streaming down my face, not knowing where I was and feeling like the neighborhood was so big and I was so far from home. The reality was that I was only about a block from home.

As we get older and look back, we realize how small our world was.

I was particularly close to my dad's mom. She divorced my dad's father when he was about 3 years old, so it was just her and Dad, and he grew up an only child. The time spent with my grandma was all about making cookies, driving in her VW bug, and listening to lots of stories about her family. She would show me old black and white photos and tell me the stories of all her brothers and sisters and her life. I probably know more about her family and their stories than anyone in my family.

Growing up on a farm in Martin, Tennessee in the early

1900's must have been challenging. She had 6 siblings, 3 brothers, and 3 sisters. She was the oldest of the girls. There were also 3 older half-brothers from her dad's previous marriage. Her stories alluded to the family not having a lot of money. She had an eighth-grade education, and from the pictures I've seen, they were all hard workers. The story as I remember it, is that her dad passed away and then her mom, meaning her youngest sister would be taken care of by 'other' family members. My grandma wouldn't have that and took Ruby in to live with her.

The way she told it, growing up it was common to be called by your middle name. At least that was the case in her family. Most of her brothers and sisters were known that way. Her given name was Dora Lorraine. She went by Lorraine, but I called her Grandma. She didn't talk about it, maybe not ever, but she was married and divorced in her twenties, living in a few midwest states during that time. Eventually she landed in the Chicago area, married again and had one son. When he was about three years old, she divorced. That's when she moved to Joliet to raise him. From what I heard, she wasn't always the easiest mom to grow up with. She was a divorcee raising a son in the 1940s and 1950s. I imagine it was long before the term "single mom" was used. It had to be challenging for her to balance work and caring for her son. I do wonder what kind of criticism she faced. She worked in the cafeteria at General Foods, proudly talking about retiring from that company. I remember a picture of her and a few co-workers behind the counter, their hair neatly kept in place with hairnets. She was a strong woman; some might have even thought her abrasive. I believe she was a compilation of her life experiences … and it didn't seem like an easy one. In those days, I imagine a confident woman who had boundaries may not have been well accepted. By the time I came around, she was in her sixties, living on her own in a small, comfortable trailer. That was Grandma's house. My early childhood is flooded with memories of time spent together there. When I stayed overnight with her, she would talk about each nick-nack on her shelf and their individual stories. There was a small pewter dog, labeled on his back side with the name "Bill". She always called him *Little Bill*. She had a treasured shell from who knows where, and a cockatoo print hanging on the wall. We had oatmeal for breakfast and made cookies in the afternoon. Being quite set in her ways, she showed me the exact *right way* to eat oatmeal. For my birthdays, she would make me German chocolate cake. She loved to cook and bake and was fantastic at both. I still stand by her cheesecake recipe as being the best I've ever had. I learned the alphabet in sign language from her; she told me she learned to sign from a co-worker along the way. She would very precisely show me how to hold my fingers to create each letter. I can still sign those letters today and I'm grateful for the foundational skills she shared with me.

She was old school; if you had a cold she'd make you a hot toddy, even if you were a young child. There was nothing petite or fancy about her. She was a presence. When at home she wore what she called her house dress. I can remember her putting on a nicer dress to go out in public, pulling up her stockings and tying them above her knee to keep them up. She might add a pin or broach to her dress for dinner or on a special occasion. And she'd neatly tie a head scarf under her chin to keep her hair in place when needed. She was proud of her Irish and English heritage. Her mother's maiden name was *Cook*, so the English descent seemed right. I'm not sure if she really was Irish, but she solidly believed she was, and so, I also believed I was. Her feet would do an 'Irish jig' while she was comfortably seated in a chair. For years, I would be sure to send her a St. Patrick's Day card to celebrate here claimed ancestry. I have fond memories of running errands in her VW Bug. Other drivers who maybe weren't moving quick enough for her were told off with her colorful phrases. She made sure I knew she had what she called a 'shillelagh' in the driver's door pocket ... just in case she needed protection. Later on, she switched out the shillelagh in her door pocket for the pistol she bought. We'd often sing in the car ... and *You Are My Sunshine* was a favorite. Even today I have a plaque with those words in my home. Once in a while, in the summer, we would stop at a convenience store for an ice cream. I usually got an orange push up, and of course she instructed me on the precise way to eat it, making sure not to let it melt and drip on me, or the car. One time when I was in kindergarten, I needed an empty can for a school father's day project, and as she was taking care of me at our house after school, she opened and drank a beer so I could have the can. (She might have let me have a sip or two.) Much of our time together was filled with her showing me old pictures illustrating the family stories. Her family connection ran deep. One grainy sepia photo showed her twin brothers, barefoot, holding candy. Apparently, her dad had taken the boys to 'have their picture made'. Their mom was unhappy that they had no shoes on and looked a bit disheveled. And there was the ever-present framed photo of her niece, *little Joanie*. Joanie's life was tragically cut short one winter's day, when she was hit by a truck as she was sledding down a hill. Forever young in the picture, with her porcelain skin, she looked every bit the angel that she was described to be, and now considered to be a guardian angel in heaven as well. Little Joanie wasn't the only angel she talked about. Not really one to go to church, she was the person who taught me to say a prayer before bed. When I would spend the night with her, together we would recite, *"Now I lay me down to sleep..."* always remembering to include, at the end, all the family members that we asked God to bless. And, of course, she would remind me that I have a guardian angel. I share the same birthday as her mother, so for my eleventh birthday, she had a locket engraved with her mother's initials and date of birth, along with mine. I also have a diamond ring she gave me. They remain treasured heirlooms of mine.

Ruby, grandma's youngest sister, (the one she raised), owned a tavern in a neighboring town. We would go there during the day. Sitting at the bar, I loved snacking on cashews served warm in a paper dixie cup. I was given coins to play the jukebox, so I could dance to the songs. Years later, my stepmother found the idea of taking a young child to a tavern inappropriate. For me, it was completely ordinary to visit my great-aunt at her business, accompanied by my grandma, and create one more memory for my memory book.

We would often visit the cemetery where her brothers, sister and little Joanie were buried. It may seem odd to some, but she already had her plot there with the family, including her headstone. She had it in place and engraved with her information, only waiting to be completed by her final date. I think that showed her capacity to make sure things were taken care of the way she wanted them. Those visits also taught me to honor and respect those that have gone before us.

When I was six years old, we moved a few hours away to another town. Now there's a new story to my life. A new house, new school, new town; living farther away from my grandparents and cousins. Changes come to our lives, and we adjust. And we have new stories to add to our lives. We get pretty comfortable with our stories. They become what we believe about ourselves and how others see us. We even label ourselves or live by the labels that others attach to us.

To keep in touch with my Grandma, I would call her

on Saturday mornings. Remember, this was back when that would have been a long-distance call, so I could only call once a week. She did come to visit us, and since we still had plenty of family in her town, we made frequent visits there also. At times, I remember taking the train with her so I could stay for a few days. And there were a couple of trips to visit her sister, a few hours away in St. Louis. I think it was when we moved that she gave me one of her night gowns to sleep in, along with my favorite pillow from her house. Imagine me as a six-year-old engulfed in my 5'9" grandma's night gown! I'd roll up the sleeves to fit while it dragged out behind me as I walked. It felt like a part of my grandma was there comforting me. I cherished that pillow for so long and it became so tattered, I finally, though begrudgingly, said farewell.

By the time I was in middle school we had moved back closer to where she lived. Her trailer had been sold by then and she rented an apartment in a house. There were three apartments upstairs, with the owners living downstairs. One time my cousin and I were sleeping over. Late in the night as we slept, there were some 'boys' making noise on the street. Well, she marched down there to inform them that she had grandkids sleeping upstairs and if they didn't quiet down, she had a pistol in the pocket of her robe and she *wasn't afraid to use it*. I think she was lucky to get away with that, but that's how she was; fearless. I never really thought of her as 'hard' or 'abrasive', to me she was the way she was and as a child it was accepted. She was fearless ... even without a pistol in her pocket. She had her own way of showing her love for her family. It wasn't until I was older that I realized what an influence she had on me, how much of her values are instilled in me; she was the most consistent, supportive adult and influence in my early years. I have been entrusted to carry with me many of her family stories that may not be known or remembered by many others - her love of baking, and yes, I believe, her strong sense of boundaries that served her well throughout her life. My experience is that blood is not always thicker than water. That many times the family members we choose have stronger bonds than those related to us by the coincidence of DNA.

Let's move on to 1971 - a whirlwind year, marked by one major change after another.

My parents were getting divorced. While we sat in the car at a red traffic light my mom announced that they were splitting up. My sister would live with Mom, and I would live with Dad. That was the entire conversation. Two sentences. We were driving home from swimming at Mom's friend's apartment complex, and I suppose we were a captive audience there in the car. In the time it took for the light to turn from green to red, and back to green ... my life had completely changed.

I had no idea on that day how different it would be in a short amount of time. I didn't even fully know what that meant. Maybe I'd heard the word here and there. Was it on a TV show? Not sure. I do remember there was a country song that I'd heard. "Our d-i-v-o-r-c-e becomes final today". They couldn't even say it - it had to be spelled out. It definitely couldn't be good.

Just a few weeks before life had been fun. I was at the state fairgrounds showing my pony. Well, we didn't actually own it. Someone that mom knew had the pony and offered to let me use it. I don't know all the arrangements, but he was moved to the stable where I took riding lessons and, for all intents and purposes, was mine. What a character he was though. If you know ponies then you know what I'm talking about. Ponies can be stubborn. We couldn't ride the whole circumference of the outdoor arena without him heading for the barn. We just cut off the circle and rode through the middle. That seemed to help. I loved my pony and riding lessons, even being part of horse shows. But my memory is tainted from one particular show, as within a week or two of being part it, I ended up sick. Very sick.

I realized after that I hadn't felt right for a while. It seemed like a long time, but being eight, a long time could have been a week or two. I was staying with my grandparents one night and they were getting fried chicken for dinner. It didn't sound good to me, but they insisted I eat … and it didn't go well. I was up out of bed and sick at their house. I didn't like being in trouble with them or being sick at their home. Another time, my aunt was staying with us, and again, I wasn't feeling well. I remember my aunt trying to help. Then one Saturday night, my parents had a cocktail party and went out to dinner with their guests, (it's what they did in the 70s, at least my parents did), and my sister was babysitting. She was only a year older, but definitely in charge. I was really sick that night; no fooling sick. But we had strict orders not to bother our parents at dinner unless it was REALLY important. That was way before cell phones. We had to call the restaurant and interrupt their dinner - not something to take lightly. But I was *really* sick. I begged my sister to call. *Nope.* She wouldn't risk the wrath of Dad if it was determined to be *not important enough*. The next day, I was still sick. It turned out that one of the previous night's dinner guests was a doctor who lived in our neighborhood, just a couple of blocks over. So, on a Sunday, my parents asked him to come take a look. I guess you could do that in the 70s. It only took a minute for him to say I needed to go to the hospital right away. Boy did that show my sister! She should have called the restaurant. She should have bothered my parents. It was *REALLY* important.

The first thing I remember about being in hospital was being in my room. I don't know how long we waited or even how I got into the room, but they needed to start an IV. For some reason the nurse was having trouble getting it into my right arm. At some point, they had asked my mom to leave the room; torturous for an eight-year-old. There were needles and repeated stabbings in my arm, along with crying and screaming. The nurses weren't nice about it. Finally, one came in and said something like, "I'll get it". She took my left arm ... and got it. Welcome to the hospital. From what I remember it was evening by then, and Mom had gone home. I was there alone for the night.

When I woke up in the morning, I couldn't tell what time it was. I used the call button to ask the nurse if my mom was there. "No". So I waited for what seemed like at least an hour, but was probably 5 minutes.... I buzzed again. "Is my mom here yet?" This continued for a while. A nurse told me that my mom would definitely come in when she arrived. I don't remember the moment my parents showed up, but for some reason the hospital staff were having trouble figuring out what to do with me. Or maybe what exactly was wrong. Eventually they decided to operate on my appendix. To my tiny ears, apparently, it was in the wrong place, so it was giving them the runaround. From my recollection, I had surgery on the Wednesday. Having arrived on Sunday had given my appendix plenty of time to create infection in my body. Surgery must have been a success because I'm here and my appendix is not, but what did remain, was the infection. They had left a tube in my body, a rubber tube sticking out of the incision, so the infection could "drain". I couldn't see it because of the dressing, but I did eventually see it, because it went home with me. It was removed at a follow-up appointment at the doctor's office and left an interesting scar. There were some fun things I remember about being in the hospital. My sister, who never let me touch anything of hers, not even a toe on the carpet of her room without yelling, let me use her cassette tape player. And even some of her cassettes! Flip Wilson was a favorite - if you don't remember him, it might be worth Googling. And even though the parent waiting game went on daily, there were some perks; presents and lots of cards from family, and my class at school. There was even one from my dad's secretary at work. I thought it was a little strange as I didn't know her. Apparently, my pattern of eating and getting sick had really drilled into my brain. My dad had a serious talk with me a couple of days after surgery about eating. I needed to eat to go home. I didn't want to eat because I thought eating would make me sick. He assured me it wouldn't. When I finally began eating, I was allowed to return home. On the way home, Mom and I stopped at the toy store. I was able to get the first members of a cowboy doll family that I'd had my eye on for a while. I remember it vividly. Over the summer, I completed the family and even collected a couple of horses for them. During my recovery, my grandma came to stay with us for a week or two, and I remember her going to the doctor with me for a follow-up appointment.

It was May when I was in hospital and school was out in June, and I was able to go back to school just for the last day or two. It felt like a really long time that I was sick, but it may have been because the summer holidays happened around the same time. I always loved summer - I think most kids do. That summer I had my pony, but couldn't ride because of the operation.

And that was the summer we were selling our house, and my parents divorced.

When you're nine time seems to take a long time. Looking back, and not really remembering the exact timing of everything, so much happened in a few months. After the divorce announcement, our house went up for sale. Mom bought a condo and Dad rented a duplex for the two of us to live in. The first day of fourth grade was moving day. My sister was able to stay home that day, but I had to go to school. This was one of many things I didn't understand. But in those days children were meant to be seen and not heard. *Do as you are told. Don't ask questions.* Parents, or at least mine, didn't explain things. Why were they even getting divorced? It didn't seem like they fought with each other. Why was I living with Dad and my sister with Mom? Did Dad lose and get stuck with me? I can remember lying under my bed, hiding, wanting to disappear. It did actually make some sense though me living with Dad; I was with Dad a lot, helping him wash the car, playing catch in the back yard or running errands with him.

But I didn't understand why I couldn't have the pony anymore. Why? Because we were moving? But he didn't *live with us,* so it made no sense to me. I was still able to take riding lessons….for a few more months.

Sometime over that summer, Dad started spending more

and more time with his secretary. You know, doing nice things for her like mowing the lawn and washing her car. In my naive world, I thought he was just being nice. One time we went to the beach with her and her two girls. It felt strange and a bit awkward to me. Soon enough, we were spending a lot of time with them. They got engaged and on Thanksgiving weekend they were married. Remember what I said about time seeming to be longer when you're young? What I found out much later in life was that my parents' divorce was final in October, about a month before the wedding. Now things really changed. The three of them moved into our two-bedroom duplex. My grandma stayed with us while they went on their honeymoon.

Again, it seemed like a long time, but really was only a few weeks, before we moved into a new house, which wasn't in my school district. I went to a different school for the second half of fourth grade. It wasn't the best school for me and I hated it. Somehow, and something I really appreciated, was that my mom realized the new school wasn't a good fit and arranged for me to go back to my old school for fifth grade. She may have said something about my emotional or mental health in her negotiations, but whatever it was, my stepmom wasn't happy about it, as she now had to drive me the further distance to school every day. But I was much happier returning to my old school.

I remember we went to church …. a lot. When I was young, we went to church in the town where my whole family lived. My grandparents went there. My cousin was in my Sunday school class. My parents and my aunt and uncle would ditch Sunday school and go out to breakfast. I couldn't believe it when I found out! When we moved towns when I was six, for whatever reason, we stopped going to church. Well, we were back. This time to a Christian church that my stepmom already went to. Sunday morning service, vacation bible school, church camp, bible stories, pot lucks. We did it all. I did it all ... like it or not. Once we were all moved into the new house and settling in together, there were a few more changes. No more riding lessons for me. Either we all took riding lessons, or none of us did. As it turned out, it was none of us. I got a new haircut too; it was the same cut as my stepsisters'. I was instructed to wear more dresses (or any) to school. Every other day was a new rule. Girls are supposed to wear dresses, in case you didn't know. On weekends, I stayed with my mom. Not every weekend, as I don't think there was an actual schedule, but whenever it worked out, I went. She had a nice two-bedroom condo, just right for her and my sister. Since I really didn't live there, I guess I didn't need a room of my own. I slept in my mom's bed with her when I was there. My sister's room was decorated to her exact liking. She even let me go in there a few times.

And that was the year that was! In just over a year, I'd had surgery and a week-long stay in the hospital, my parents got divorced, they sold our house, Dad got married again, and the new wife and kids moved in with us. He bought a new house so we moved again, and I went to a new school, and then back to my old school. No more riding horses, dressing or looking like myself … but we did go to church - I have to say, sometimes I do ok on the Biblical Jeopardy questions.

Which Came First…Cinderella Or The Egg?

In the story of Cinderella, Cindy is left to deal with her mean stepmother (and stepsisters of course), after the death of her father. But which came first…the fairy tale or real life? I've witnessed this story play out in life many times. Dad marries a new woman who, for whatever reason is less than nice to his children from a previous relationship. Whether it's jealousy, insecurity, or something else, the new wife just can't seem to be nice to the kids. And it doesn't help that frequently, the dad takes a back seat in parenting. (At least when I was growing up this was the case.). The old model was that women, of course, know best when raising children, so the man sits his ass in his comfy chair to watch the game, oblivious to what is going on in his own household. He is so enamored with the new wife, she must be good to his kids - *she must know what she's doing!* And to give him the benefit of the doubt, as time progresses, he wants to keep peace in the relationship and his world, so he either goes along with her or truly doesn't realize what is going on. (Maybe because the new wife doesn't let him see it.) In my case, I'm sure this was in play. At one point, when they were contemplating separation, blame was placed on my stepmom feeling unloved by me, rather than on her wandering eye. In some situations, if the new wife only has one child of her own perhaps, she can't understand why her stepchild isn't like her own. Maybe if she had more than one biological child, she might realize that no two people are the same. I also firmly believe that by the time a child is five, they know the rules of the road in their household and hopefully follow them. So, imagine when, at say 9 years old, after the rules being firmly embedded in them by their parents, their whole life changes. Not only have their parents split, but they find themselves with a new stepmom, and new rules. It would be like moving to a new country and driving on the other side of the road, with signs in a different language! Of course, the stepmom will want her own rules to be followed but think about the major adjustment for the children. It seems that some of this has evolved and we are trying to be more aware and compassionate. I've heard parents of blended families use the term "bonus" son or daughter rather than "step". Hopefully, this is more than just words. I'm not saying this is always the case. There are plenty of families that are able to embrace the mix of all the kids really well. It's just that I have frequently noticed the opposite and can't help but wonder which was first? Does life mimic the fairy tale or does the fairy tale mimic life?

CHAPTER 2
TEENAGE YEARS

August is a busy birthday time for people I know. One of them is my stepmom. It has been years since I've spoken to her since she and my dad divorced more than 30 years ago, but the other day I remembered that her birthday was coming up. It made me think about her and the years I spent growing up in my dad's house with her. What I realized is that she taught me many things. She taught me lots about cooking and baking. I am a great pie maker because of her ... yes it's home made crust! Oh, and laundry... boy did she teach me about doing laundry and ironing! Doing at least three loads of laundry every other day for about five years makes you pretty good! It wasn't just household stuff though. I learned how I didn't want to treat people, particularly children. As a parent I knew I didn't want to hit my kids with spatulas, brushes, or wooden spoons. She also showed me what insecurity and jealousy look like. Her *un-acceptance* of me and attempts to form me into what she wanted, gave me a strong belief in individuality, both supporting that in others and embracing my own. I learned about manipulation and how to tell someone what they wanted to hear (even if it wasn't true) to avoid being hit. Along the way, she introduced me to a different religion, and hypocrisy, and that people in glass houses shouldn't throw stones. And about being judgmental; telling me once that I would go to hell for not going to church. She taught me the value of being quiet and not allowing people to always know what you are thinking. Living with her showed me that some men will do anything to avoid confrontation with their wife. I learned to work for and save my money, then to spend it wisely on clothes or a down payment on a car. All of this made me stronger. It made me autonomous. It taught me to set goals and not to act rashly, but to plan and wait for the right time to leave an unpleasant situation. She will probably never know how grateful I am for the things she taught me. I won't see her or even speak to her on her special day, but I hope she has a happy birthday.

Getting into Trouble
Oooh interesting. So reframe "getting into trouble" and ask yourself what it really means. Getting into trouble with who? By whose standards? To which illusion? What you're

really describing is fear of judgement, but we can ask the same questions in that regard too. Judged by who? In which world? Under what messed up societal conditioning has this fear even become apparent? What if you chose to remove yourself from the illusion entirely and imagined yourself so full of love and light that nothing irritated you or angered you.

Of course, the first set of rules were from my parents. Living by their rules and not getting into trouble to avoid being yelled at, spanked, etc. For a long time, I have said that as children we learn the "rules of the house" very well by the age of 4 or 5. By that age they are really ingrained in your behavior. No doubt there are those who don't play well under those rules or break them. I definitely did this. The curve ball came when my parents divorced, my dad remarried and new rules were implemented. I learned to play by the new rules. These crossed over to suppressing my personality and individuality. I learned to "survive" under these circumstances and even manipulate them.

Through my teenage years, I remember playing over in my head how my mom and dad had drawn straws; how they both wanted my sister … and Dad lost. This is how your brain works as a child. But that really wasn't what happened – there were no long straws – the straws were all short. For a while, I thought I would be better off at Mom's but then, my sister did say that living with Mom's new husband was no picnic either.

This has really been a key that has developed my core belief in supporting individuality in people. One of the expectations of my parents was to get good grades. It was expected, however, they didn't do anything to be supportive of that. For whatever reason, luckily, I was self-motivated and able to maintain good grades. There is also a level of self-satisfaction along with this. Somewhere in growing up, I also learned that I hated getting yelled at or in trouble when I didn't do anything wrong. Once my stepmother slapped me in the face for telling the truth. She didn't believe it was the truth, but it was. I felt I was punished for doing the right thing. This is still with me and a trigger!

A family member acting up, especially in a small town ... shows up as me being part of it. I'm seen as "in trouble" by association. In trying to fly under the radar and stay out of trouble in that household, I realized that if I graduated from high school early, I could get out of my home situation ... early. I learned the "rules" of how to graduate early, what credits were required, what classes had to be taken, and during what grade level. And I did it – I graduated one year early from high school.

In 1976, at the age of fourteen, I went to Finland with my grandparents.

Both my grandparents, on my mom's side of the family, are Finnish and still had relatives back in Finland. It was a big deal travelling overseas back then and even communicating. They wrote letters back and forth to their relatives, and it was a couple of years earlier that I'd heard they were going, because they had to plan well in advance. I'd asked, "If I save my money to pay for my ticket, can I go?" And everyone agreed, probably thinking I'd never save enough, but I saved my money and was able to experience an amazing trip with them. I had a very generous great aunt. She was generous to everyone in her life, and always gave us money for our birthdays and at Christmas. She knew I really wanted to go, and so she gave me a little extra here and there to save. But every birthday, every Christmas, anytime I got money, it went in the bank for my trip.

Although born in the States, my grandfather grew up in Finland, as his parents passed away when he was young, so his relatives took care of him. He came back to the States as a young adult. There's a big Finnish community Minnesota and in Northern Illinois, where they were from.

That ended up by being their last trip to Finland. I've now been to Finland three times; once with my grandparents and then with my son in 2004, and again with him in 2006. And we've had Finnish relatives come and stay with us as well. I'm really close with a couple of my Finnish relatives.

I was eighteen I had moved to California and then off to college. My first car was a Pontiac Firebird! Everyone knew I wanted a Firebird …. It was no secret. I had been working a good part-time job while I was in high school, earning double time on the weekends, so Dad said if I saved up for half of the down payment he would match my funds for the the car. I would have to make the payments on the car loan. Talk about manifesting – I had a picture up on the wall from the dealer for months! I didn't get the fancy Transam, and my car didn't have air conditioning – but I loved it. I was still in high school when I bought the car, so I'm sure most people thought my parents had bought it for me ... but it was mine and I was really proud of my very first car.

It wasn't classed as a shared family car, but there were times I'd drop my stepmom to work, and I was definitely given the job of picking my stepsister up from school. Funny thing was that I had gone to that same school and either walked or rode my bike. We only lived a few blocks away. It caused a small issue when a couple of years later I wanted to move California – but hey – I'd been paying the repayments – it was my car! Dad stepped in for me in that moment and insisted it was my car, as I paying for it!

After graduating, I moved out of Dad's and lived with my best friends' family. They were moving back to California and invited me to go with them, but I had a boyfriend and a job, and a fantastic car, so I chose to stay and move in with Mom for a while.

But I didn't stay there for long! When my sister returned from college, the Queen of Everything, I decided that California was the place for me.

CHAPTER 3
TWENTIES AND IDENTITY CRISIS

When I was deciding on college, I wanted to attend Moorpark College in California because they offered a graphics program. However, my best friend, whom I lived with, was going to school in Idaho, and I didn't have strong guidance from my parents. So, I decided to follow my friend to Idaho, even though it wasn't my first choice. Interestingly, Idaho was a good example of trying to force something that doesn't fit.

In my first semester, I tried to make the best of it, taking art classes that I thought would be close to graphics. I enrolled in a drawing class, a lettering class (which I quickly dropped), and art history. I was only an average student in drawing, surrounded by some truly talented artists. I struggled with perspective drawing assignments—I must have missed some crucial instructions because I couldn't grasp the concept at all. Honestly, I was ready to drop out by the time winter break arrived and return to California to attend Moorpark.

But my friend's parents encouraged me to go back and take classes I enjoyed, and focus on general education. So, I went back for another semester, branching out to subjects like photography, biology, and astronomy. The astronomy class, a last-minute addition, turned out to be a surprise passion - I loved every bit of it.

After finishing out the year in Idaho, I finally transferred to Moorpark College to pursue graphics. Back then, the technology was so different; we worked with huge typesetting machines, cut and pasted photos by hand, and even ran printing presses with ink rollers. I really enjoyed it, especially my instructor, who was a real character.

One memory from Idaho stayed with me: in my drawing class, we once had to draw an old, beat-up tricycle in pen and ink. I kept that drawing rolled up for years, and my husband eventually found it. As a birthday surprise, he had it framed, and that little piece of Idaho became a special memory.

It was in my Twenties, when I learned to fly. When I went to get my pilot's licence, everybody was saying, "Oh, people always want to take flying lessons, and then they run out of money." And I didn't look at it that way. Just as when I went to Finland, I saved the money first. I saved money, put it in the bank, and then took flying lessons. I knew how to make it happen.

I had to take ground school to learn about the mechanics of the airplane, the science of flight, and the FAA rules. There are scientific laws at play in order for a plane to fly. A certain speed must be reached to take off. A certain speed must be maintained to land…or gravity will take effect too soon and the plane will crash. These laws can be pushed and that's when aerobatics or even space flight are reached. Even working with clay to create pottery there are rules to obtain the best results. Otherwise things may collapse, explode or look like crap. So here's the bottom line… There are rules in place. Societal rules, scientific laws, universal laws, etc. For the most part these laws need to be followed to obtain the best results possible. BUT…when you know the rules well….this is where you can also learn to push the limits of the laws to really be creative or disruptive.

CHAPTER 4
IN THE MIDST OF BECOMING

In my twenties, life was a mess of trial and error, independence and missteps, all pieced together with moments of hard-won resilience. I found myself learning not only who I was but who I didn't want to be. My life in those years was defined by choices that were sometimes right, sometimes painfully wrong, but always uniquely mine.

Leaving Idaho to return to California, I enrolled in the graphics program at Moorpark College, which felt like a breath of fresh air after the wrong-fit art program I'd tried up north. Graphics back then was painstaking work—typesetters, metal plates, ink smudges, and all—but there was something about the tactile nature of it that grounded me. I could pour myself into perfecting the smallest details, each line and form offering control when so much in my life felt beyond it. A professor there recognized something in me that I hadn't yet acknowledged, encouraging me to explore my potential, giving me the confidence to press forward.

Outside of school, I was learning to juggle adult responsibilities, not just for financial reasons but to prove to myself that I could. I landed a job as a receptionist at a financial planning firm through a church connection. It felt like a lifeline, a step toward stability, and even if I was thrown in without much direction, I adapted. Soon, I found myself working in the limited partnerships department, keeping track of investments and client information. My boss became a mentor, and the job gave me purpose. But that purpose came with a price—my world was tangled up with people from church, a web of expectations and invisible boundaries that grew taut when I began dating someone outside of the fold. My relationship went against the rules of the family I lived with, and after months of broken curfews and growing tension, they asked me to leave.

At nineteen, I was abruptly on my own. I found a room to rent, thrown into an awkward shared living situation with a middle-aged landlord and another tenant who felt more like strangers than housemates. It wasn't ideal—my belongings were crammed into a single room, and I had no true sense of privacy. There was a night when someone stole gas out of my car, leaving me stranded, financially tight, and feeling as if the world was conspiring against me. Each setback seemed to compound, adding weight to the load I carried. But even then, there was a small part of me that knew I was growing stronger, learning to fend for myself in ways I hadn't before.

In the middle of all this upheaval, life threw me a curveball. I found out I was pregnant, a revelation that filled me with an overwhelming mix of fear, shame, and confusion. My boss was the first person I confided in, and I later called my parents, who urged me to wait before seeing a doctor. I was naïve, terrified, and so young. Then, before I could fully process it, I miscarried. The experience left me relieved and grieving all at once, a confusing tangle of emotions that I didn't know how to untangle. It was a turning point, a moment that forced me to confront the reality of my life choices and accept that my path would not be straightforward.

I kept moving forward—school, work, and my relationship all demanding more than I sometimes felt I could give. Eventually, seeking stability, I returned to Illinois, hoping family support would make things easier. But job prospects were slim, and without income, my plans to stand on my own feet stalled. After months of frustration, I called my former boss in California, who offered me my job back. I returned to California, moving in with my boyfriend and beginning a cycle of shared apartments, financial tightness, and hand-me-down furniture. Our first place didn't even come with a stove; we saved up for one, making do with a camp stove in the meantime. Each meal cooked on that tiny propane burner was a reminder of the life we were barely holding together.

Over time, the cracks in my relationship widened. I new it was unstable. I talked to my sister about returning to Illinois, again, not knowing what else to do. My boyfriend overheard the conversation and the next thing I knew he had bought a ring. When he asked me to marry him my heart sank. My head said no but my mouth said yes.

Money was always tight, and when I lost my job, my employer refused to pay me for the vacation days and sick time I'd accumulated. I was furious. For the first time, I pushed back, filing a complaint with the labor board, winning the case and receiving the money I was due. It was a small but essential victory, one that helped me see that I could stand up for myself, even when it wasn't easy.

But as I gained strength, I saw more clearly the flaws in my marriage. We had settled into a pattern, choosing security over connection, staying together out of habit rather than love. Christmas became the turning point. An argument turned physical, leaving me bruised and shaken. Standing there in our living room, I knew I couldn't continue. I wasn't going to compromise my safety, my self-worth, for the sake of maintaining the facade. This time, I chose to leave, to put myself first, even if it meant starting from scratch.

I kept the house, borrowing money from my mother and grandmother to buy out my ex-husband's share. I rented out spare rooms to cover the mortgage, learning the ropes of property management with each new tenant. The experiences were rarely ideal; one tenant bounced checks, leaving me to chase her down for rent, another was unreliable, but I was learning. Each small struggle taught me how to hold my ground, how to protect what was mine.

In the midst of all this, I sought new ways to ground myself, discovering a passion for flying. I took lessons. Taking to the skies was more than just a hobby; it was freedom, control, and exhilaration. Soloing on my 25th birthday felt like a declaration that I was stronger, more capable than I'd ever believed. I was making choices for myself, learning to balance risk with reward, and growing more confident with each flight. Flying became a symbol of my independence, a reminder that I could rise above the challenges I faced on the ground.

As I worked my way through jobs—receptionist, bookkeeper, real estate agent, I discovered the rhythms of independence. Financial stability was hard-won, and for a long time, I was piecing together a life through sheer determination. When I finally landed a job close to home, my world felt a little more manageable. I had a five-minute commute, enough time to go home for lunch, and I'd even started dating again. In my small, grounded ways, I was building a life.

I held on to that lesson as my twenties progressed. Each job, each relationship, each setback became part of the story I was crafting. By the time I turned thirty, I had collected a lifetime's worth of lessons. I had learned how to assert myself, how to navigate relationships, and how to find stability within myself rather than seeking it in others. My twenties were a chapter of discovery, a time of forging my own path and redefining what it meant to build a life on my own terms.

Looking back, I see a young woman who was finding herself piece by piece, shaping her own identity with each decision, each heartbreak, each victory. I was messy, imperfect, but wholly committed to becoming. And as I entered my thirties, I knew I had something more than just memories. I had the strength to create the life I truly wanted, unbound by anyone else's expectations but my own.

CHAPTER 5
DISCOVERY AND RECKONING

What would you do if you discovered that the person who should be the most protective of you, the most loving towards you, actually lied to you your whole life? On top of that, they betrayed and abandoned you, neglecting your needs and feelings. What would you do if that person was your mother? What if, at 43 years old, you discovered that your whole life was a lie?

The story of your life, as you were told, and fully believed, was completely untrue. There was no reason not to believe the story, it was a common one, nothing unusual that would raise a flag or lead someone to question it. And that's the beauty of it. The power of a good story. Nothing out of the norm to question. Because the real story is full of things that people will question. Funny how we can accept a good story without batting an eye, fully believe it. Swallow it hook, line, and sinker. But the truth…oh that's what is unbelievable. Where the questions come up. Well, you know the old saying … the truth is stranger than fiction.

The Secrets We Hold

They say blood ties us, binds us into families, but what happens when that very blood begins to unravel the truth? The quiet suspicions I held for so many years were born out of the smallest details, fragments of conversations that lingered in my mind. I was an adult before I started piecing together the reality that the man I called "Dad" wasn't my father. Yet, the full truth was something I could never have prepared for.

The first hint surfaced during a casual conversation. My sister, who was pregnant at the time, was discussing her blood type with my dad. She mentioned being O, Dad was also O, and our mother, as far as he knew, was O as well. But I wasn't. I was type A. It doesn't take a biology degree to understand that O plus O doesn't make A. I brushed it aside, tried to reason it away, but that small detail was like a burr caught in my mind. I began to wonder about things I hadn't questioned before.

I couldn't go directly to my mother - not at first. I tried to approach it sideways, in the quiet moments, asking innocently about her blood type, but she dodged me, offering vague answers. She even got angry once or twice, which only heightened my suspicion. Still, I never imagined the truth would be what it was. In my mind, maybe she'd had an affair, a moment she regretted. It wasn't until years later that I found out what had really happened.

Finally, seven years later, as she sat across from me, she admitted that my biological father wasn't the man I'd grown up knowing as my dad. My real father was someone she'd once worked with, someone who had taken what wasn't his to take. My entire life shifted in that moment, the ground beneath me feeling as if it had been made of sand, sliding away. To say I was stunned was an understatement.

As she continued talking, she explained how this man, had not only threatened her job but my father's too. I imagined her carrying this secret for decades, a truth that would fracture her image in our small Michigan town if it ever came to light. For twelve years, she'd served as Village President, the embodiment of success, a woman of standing in a tight-knit community where everyone knew everyone else's business - or at least thought they did. She was woven into the fabric of that town, and I understood why she might hold on to this story. She couldn't risk her carefully built life unravelling.

The Truth of It All

A landslide of emotions engulfed me as I walked through the hospital doors to my car. I finally had confirmation. After seven years of wondering, I finally knew. My drive home was a swirl of anger, betrayal, disappointment, anxiety, topped off with confusion - all running through my head and body. My main question had been answered but that only opened the door to a flood of fresh questions. Walking into my house from the drive home the only thing I could do was open the freezer and grab a 1/2 gallon of ice cream. Those emotions had to be fed. Even with the years of speculation that you think might be a buffer zone, and might have prepared me for that day, I didn't know how it would hit when it finally did. What was confirmed that day was that the man I knew as my father, was not. Who was? What happened? How was I raised by a man who was not my father and his second wife? There were so many questions in my head as my family tree crumbled. The genetic traits that I thought were shared with my father, myself, and my children, in fact, were not. Stories can be told, or hidden, for years, even decades, but there is no story that trumps the facts of blood type and DNA. And that day, I had all the facts. I didn't know the whole story and wasn't sure I ever would. In the following days I knew I had to have some guidance about my next steps and how to try to handle my emotions. The best I could do for myself at that time was talk to a counselor. By the time of my appointment, I had already written a letter asking for answers. It was filled with anger. I was angry and I did not care if it came through in my written words. I did not care if my contempt during those days came across in my questions. After 43 years of lies, I felt entitled to an explanation. To my surprise, I was given the answers about a week later, both what had happened and who my biological father is. All the years of wondering and speculation hadn't prepared me for what I heard. Even though I was grateful to know the truth and have answers, this only began what would be years of working through what I now knew. There were so many layers of emotions for me to deal with.

Through the magic of technology, I was able to see pictures of him; my biological father. I could see the physical traits that I had in common with him. How could I have similar features to someone like him? Initially I wrote him a letter, saying that there had been an incident and I was born 9 months after. I wanted him to know that I existed. He actually wrote back to me, not acknowledging or denying anything. I wondered why he would even bother responding. For some reason he mentioned in his letter that he'd had some recent identity theft. Wow…that really gave me a chuckle. Find out when you're 43 that everything you've believed about yourself and your family wasn't true and then talk to me about identity theft!

For years, my mother and I barely spoke. The resentment was like a shadow between us, persistent and unyielding. I tried to move past it, tried to forgive her, but the anger lingered.

The relationship I had with both of my parents became unhinged. The already existing arm's length relationship with my mom was stretched further, by my choice, of placing stronger boundaries to protect myself. Looking at my childhood from a new perspective, changed the relationship with my dad as well. It wasn't the same ... knowing the truth. I know he did the best he could given his choices and circumstances, and I believe that he genuinely thought I was his daughter.

In the years following this revelation, I would occasionally make an effort to connect with my mom. I came home near Thanksgiving to help her with her knee surgery. I stayed at her home for a few days to care for her. That visit was a test, both of my patience and my ability to forgive. During one quiet evening, I listened to a gratitude podcast. The episode featured an interview with a former athlete who, after a tragic car accident, had to give up his dreams. Instead of dwelling on what he'd lost, he spoke about finding gratitude in the unexpected. He was thankful for the accident, which had reshaped his life in ways he hadn't foreseen.

The message was that he was able to find the gratitude in his circumstances. And the challenge to the listeners was to find gratitude in our own personal experiences. As I lay there in my mother's home, that message resonated deeply, Thinking about that challenge, Seriously, what gratitude could I possibly find in the circumstances of my birth? For so long, I had been carrying resentment, unable to forgive her for not speaking up. But in that quiet moment, an answer finally came to me. I realized that if any other two people had been my parents, I would not be me. It was as simple and profound as that. It finally came to me. This was the DNA that had shaped me, and if I could honor that, I could finally let go of some of the anger.

It came down to science. In case you don't know, the odds of your existence and you being who you are, is 1 in 400 quadrillion. Each one of us is literally a miracle! That was a huge aha moment for me. It really was a turning point in acceptance and helping me to find peace with my circumstances.

Connecting with my half-brother was another step on this journey. It began with a blunt Father's Day card I'd sent to my biological father. I didn't sign it with affection; I wasn't reaching out in kindness. I wanted him to remember that I existed, that there was someone out there who would always be part of his story. Years later, my half-brother reached out after discovering that card among his father's things, and we connected for the first time. It was strange and surreal to meet him, this man who was family but felt like a stranger.

We met in Chicago, then again in New Jersey, forging a relationship that was hesitant yet healing in its own way. In the years since, our connection has remained distant but meaningful - a way for me to grasp a part of my own identity that had been kept hidden for so long.

But the surprises kept coming. There was one strange memory that returned to me - a whisper of intuition from when I was a child, perhaps the most startling part of this journey was the realization that in some subconscious way, I had always known. I remember being ten years old, sitting in church one Sunday morning with my dad, stepmother and stepsisters. It was during a quiet moment, the kind where the mind drifts, that I heard a voice in my mind as clearly as if it were spoken aloud: "He's is not your dad, and your real dad is not a good man." I dismissed it, chalked it up to a stray thought, something that made no sense. It wasn't until years later that I remembered that moment and realized that some part of me had always known.

That memory haunts me, but it also brings me comfort. I was somehow prepared for this truth, long before it ever reached me.

The journey to heal and forgive has not been linear. I carried anger for years, my silence becoming a prison of its own. I told myself that not sharing my story was a form of loyalty, a way to protect my mother. But in withholding it, I was denying my own truth. Writing it now, I feel a freedom I hadn't thought possible. There's a strength in releasing it, a way to let the secrets live in the open where they can no longer control me. Writing it now feels like honoring my own journey, a way of bringing the hidden parts of my life into the light.

This story is not just about me—it's about anyone who has faced hidden truths, who has lived in the shadow of someone else's choices. I hope that by sharing it, I can offer a light for others navigating their own journeys, a way to reclaim their lives from the stories others have told about them.

The final stage of healing, I've come to realize, is in sharing. I tell my story not for pity or revenge, but because it is a truth that needs to be spoken. Every person deserves to know where they come from, to honor their own path. And if, in telling this story, I can help even one person navigate their own hidden truths, then I've found the purpose in this journey. After all, it's not just about the secrets we hold - it's about the freedom that comes when we finally let them go.

The View from the Other Side

A funny thing happened … Not surprising really to hear that in the middle of this book … or my life. But the timing of this couldn't be ignored. Right as I am writing my story, this story, the one that includes me discovering that my dad wasn't my dad, I was given the opportunity to view that from another angle. From the other side, if you will. What I have come to see is that there are many people who are searching for family members. Looking to connect with their ancestors, heritage, or genetics for medical reasons. Wanting to potentially 'fill in the gaps' of who they are. Some have been given up for adoption and are looking for their biological parents. Some are parents looking for children who were adopted by others long ago. Some have been told somewhere along the way that their 'known' parent or parents are actually *not* their biological parent or parents. Some find surprises when building out their family tree. Secrets have been kept.

Stories have long been told. The people keeping secrets and telling stories don't want them to be unraveled. They will often go to great lengths to avoid the truth. Even when shown the facts of DNA testing. My biological father dismissed the science of DNA when presented to him. It's not easy to find out that the parent who raised you isn't actually your parent. It's also not easy to discover that you have a child you had no knowledge of after 20, 30, or 40 years. Every situation is unique, but no doubt each comes with their own emotions to navigate, regardless of which side you find yourself on.

Safe Harbour

It doesn't feel safe at times. Sometimes it feels like a ship on the ocean susceptible to the changing winds, damaging waves, and unknown that lies below. Just when it seems that calm waters and clear sailing is in store, an unexpected storm blows in, making you question your navigations skills and tools, maybe even your vessel itself, and hoping you have the experience behind you to ride out the storm. Every storm is different. At times it's best to make it to what appears to be a safe harbor and shelter for a time. Refuel, restock, refresh and make any repairs. It could be time to reassess your crew. Is it a supportive group? Loyal? Can they bring what's necessary to continue on the journey with you? Is there a sense of community? Will they be with you for both the glassy seas and the choppy waves?

"You are the captain of your own ship; don't let anyone else

Laura Muirhead

take the wheel" - Michael Josephson

CHAPTER 6
MIDLIFE TRANSFORMATION

As we've earlier explored, stories are so powerful.

I was born into a story that I was the youngest child of two parents, a mother and a father, and I had an older sister. This was my family. There were also grandparents, aunts, uncles and cousins, and as previously mentioned, I was particularly close to my father's mother, though she never knew we weren't connected by blood. Much of my early childhood was spent with her, and she told me stories. Stories of her family. Many of them were told over and over through those years. One story she told, was that my grandfather was caught up with a hooker. I didn't know what that meant, and she knew I was too young to know because she would say to me, "you don't know what that means, but some day you will". When your grandmother says that to you, you keep that word in your memory for *some day*. Anyway, that was the story that she told about her ex-husband and his wife. The wife he married after they had divorced. The one he was still married to when she told me that story. Do I believe that she was a hooker? No. Unless you look at it like she somehow hooked him in and stole him away from my grandma, which is what I believe my grandma believed. Maybe it was true, I'll never know for sure. So these were stories I was told. My immediate family was my dad, mom and sister. And I had no reason to believe otherwise. There's nothing unusual or questionable about this story, a midwestern family of four, parents that worked at comfortable jobs, kids that went to school, played outside or rode their bikes with friends. We love stories. We love to tell them and we love to hear them. We laugh at them and we learn from them. Sometimes we believe them and sometimes we don't. Sometimes they are true and sometimes they are not. But what about the stories that we tell ourselves? We love to tell them. We love to believe them. We love to think they're true. But sometimes they are not. Stories are so incredibly powerful that we can convince ourselves of anything. Some people are so good at telling stories that they can convince *others* of just about anything. Maybe you want so badly to believe something that you will find only what you want to put a good story together to support your belief. That's also true of the opposite. If you want to believe something or someone is bad, you can put that story together as well. And sometimes we want to ignore something that was so bad that we create a really convincing story that didn't actually happen as a substitute, another better story in place of the one we are suppressing. We believe the new story and so do those who hear the story. This is my story, told from my view point and my experiences. Some people reading this might find it unbelievable.

Another fun story I have, is that I had a friend that played the lottery every Wednesday and Saturday. Back then there weren't all the games, no national ones like Powerball and Mega Millions, the lottery was run by each state. It was one game, Lotto. I used to joke with my friend because he played it so often. I was like, "give me your $5. I'll give you two dollars back every time, and you'll still be ahead of where you are now with playing the lotto." He didn't go for it. Don't get me wrong, I would play once in a while when I got an urge. Usually it would be for a birthday, a holiday and especially New Years. Who wouldn't want to start the new year with a lottery win? That Saturday, New Year's Day, my best friend and I went out to dinner and a movie. I can remember talking at dinner about our plans for the year. She had weddings and events already on her calendar. When she finished sharing her plans with me she asked what I had planned. At the time I was pregnant with my second child, so I said, I didn't have any big plans except for having my baby in the summer. A few months earlier though, there had been some talk about moving from California to Illinois, where I grew up and my family still lived. We had even had a chat with a local realtor. Those ideas were put on hold, as the timing didn't seem right .... But little did I know what was to come!

A Journey Through Fortunes and Family

Some people think that winning the lottery would change everything, would answer all the questions life could throw at you. But as I look back on my life, lottery win and all, I realize how little it changes what matters. Money only amplifies what's already there: the quirks of family, the twists of relationships, the need to understand ourselves. What it did give me, though, was perspective - a view of how things we think are pivotal can be simply a passing season, one more part of a lifetime of change and growth.

In 1994, I held a lottery ticket with the numbers that would change the trajectory of my life. I still remember the day I bought it, in a rush of routine errands after Christmas. My daughter and I had just flown back home to California, and my husband was off on a work trip. There we were, checking off a list of mundane things: the bank, the drug store, the office. As I walked into the drug store, I noticed the small, hopeful sign advertising the New Year's Day draw. I bought the ticket out of impulse.

The next day, the newspaper showed me a combination of numbers that looked eerily familiar. I double-checked, and then triple-checked, and finally, with hands shaking, I whispered the words to myself... I won the lottery.

I held the secret for a day or so, too stunned to even begin to understand what it meant. The next day was surreal as we headed to the lottery office, filled with equal parts of disbelief and anticipation, signing forms, securing the ticket, wondering what, if anything, would ever be the same again.

The prize, $6.7 million over 20 years, seemed like something out of a movie. But movies don't show what happens when life keeps moving around a win like that. I didn't want fame, didn't want people to see me any differently than they already did. Still, life began to shift, subtly at first, then gradually in ways I couldn't ignore. Some friends were thrilled, others saw only an opportunity. Family dynamics, especially, took on a new, tense energy.

For some, the win became a reason to ask for help, to seek out the financial support they felt entitled to. I wanted to give back, wanted to use this chance to make a difference in lives beyond my own - but I also knew that sometimes, help had to be earned.

My sister was perhaps the hardest to navigate. I think she came to believe that she deserved the win more than I did, that fate had somehow misdirected the windfall. I believe in her mind, it was her turn to win, her turn to have the luck I'd stumbled upon. For years it seemed she may have held onto a bitterness I could never quite understand. When she borrowed money, I tried to help in ways that felt fair, like advancing credit that she could repay. She wanted something simpler; no strings attached. And I learned that sometimes, helping can hurt, too, when people expect more than you can reasonably give.

Beyond the money, though, the lottery became something else entirely. It became a chance to learn about giving, to set my own boundaries and figure out what I truly valued. I donated quietly, not for show, but to causes and people who, like me, were willing to work toward something bigger. To this day, I have a simple rule for giving; *I will help those already helping themselves, those who have the resolve to reach for their dreams even when it's hard.* And through this, I found a kind of peace, a way to honor the blessings life had handed me while staying true to who I was.

The years after the win were a whirlwind, opening businesses, moving to new homes and taking changes we may not have taken without the lotto win.

And there was my head surgery!

Around 1998, I was showing horses. For as long as I could remember, I'd had a lump on the left side of my forehead. It didn't really bother me except for the random times it might get hit by a hairbrush. But with showing horses and wearing tight hats, it would hurt from the pressure of the hat, so I decided to have a doctor take a look. It turned out to be an aneurism; a group of blood vessels. Removing required a neurologist and a plastic surgeon. There were questions about how long it had been there and if it had grown. Did I fall? Did I hit my head? I didn't have the answers. Like

I said it had been there for as long as I could remember but looking back at pictures, it hadn't *always* been there. It did seem to have slowly gotten larger though. The only thing I can think of was getting hit with a baseball when I was about 7 or 8. On weekends I would ask Dad to play baseball with me, usually after he'd watched the Cubs' game on TV. If I pestered him enough, we would go in the back yard and play catch or he'd pitch to me so I could practice batting. That is exactly what got me hit in the head. The ball wasn't thrown hard, but it sure hurt anyway when it hit me. Neither one of us thought anything more about it. Not until I wanted something done with the bump and all the questions. It's the only thing I can think might have caused it. The neurologist had shown me the titanium plate he was going to replace the bump with. It looked like a snowflake; well, bigger than a snowflake but the shape of one. He had some concern about my left sinus but wouldn't know the outcome until surgery. The morning of surgery, I drove to the hospital. The kids had school so I took myself. The nurses seemed surprised. At one point the anesthesiologist came in to talk to me. He was surprised how calm I was ... "considering the procedure". I wondered if there was more to be worried about. You know, more than having my head opened up and a metal plate screwed to my skull. Turns out he thought I was a different patient that was having a tumor removed. Nope. Just a new plate installed. Surgery seemed to go well, I mean, I woke up and all that. They settled me into a room. At some point my ex-husband was there, and stayed until the kids needed him after school. I stayed in the hospital for one or two nights, but what I do remember about it, is sleeping a lot … and taking some pretty serious pain killers. I also remember my ex having to leave for a work trip soon after I was home. Sooner than I would have liked. Sooner than I was ready for, considering I needed to take care of the kids. The good news was that they didn't have to shave my hair. I was amazed and thankful to the plastic surgeon. This was also a plus in that I could wear a hat for a couple of days when I was out of the house. It wasn't lost on me that I was mostly on my own for this, and to some extent, it reminded of the experience of having my appendix removed when I was young. When my sister had surgery to remove a cyst a few years earlier, my mom had stayed with her for several days. She didn't even have kids. But here I was after this surgery with two kids and no mom.

My marriage had already begun to fray during this time, and by 2001, we separated, each of us heading down a different path.

My ex and I got divorced, but it was incredibly amicable. We stayed friends and always prioritized our kids. If they had a concert or a game, we'd sit together, so much so that people didn't even realize we were divorced. Sometimes our daughter would sit between us at our son's baseball games, and people would look surprised when they learned we were no longer married. It was essential to me that my kids didn't experience the turbulence I went through in my own childhood.

Looking back, there were many factors that contributed to our separation. The bread store was a big one - when the business failed, I was blamed, as it was my idea. Ultimately, over time, I felt like I was doing everything by myself.

Then there's a funny twist to my story. I actually met my current husband back in the late 1980s, just around the same time I met my second husband. He was living in New Jersey, and I was in California. We met on New Year's Eve, and we kept in touch briefly before life took us in different directions. Many years later, in 2006, I had a dream that reminded me of him. I tracked him down online, gave him a call, and, after a bit of catching up, we started emailing.

After about a year of sending each other the odd email, things picked up, and he invited me to visit him. It worked out that my kids were with their dad that weekend, so I flew out to New Jersey, where we explored New York City and Atlantic City. We had an incredible time, and from that point, things moved quickly. By Valentine's Day of 2008, we were engaged, and we married that July.

Looking back, it feels like everything came full circle. We hadn't forgotten about each other, and reconnecting was just a matter of the right timing. Sometimes, life has a way of bringing people back together when the moment is finally right. That second beginning felt like destiny, a story I hadn't seen coming, as if life was nudging me back toward the man I was meant to find all along.

Looking back, I can see how the lottery win marked one chapter, but only a chapter, of a far richer story. Money came and went, but the real wealth was in the experiences that shaped me, in the relationships that deepened, the self-knowledge that grew from learning to let go of what didn't serve me. Today, I know that winning wasn't about the number of zeros on a check; it was about understanding what matters, about finding peace amidst the noise and joy in the quiet moments of life's beautiful, messy journey.

Over the years, I've gathered a wealth of experience in both business and real estate. I've bought and sold houses, navigated the intricacies of property management, and found a true passion in real estate transactions. At one point, I even held a real estate license and worked alongside a property manager, learning the ins and outs of the industry from the ground up.

Going into the bread store business, and owning a barn property with a rental house on, was another adventure altogether. It taught me the practicalities of being a business owner and landlord, adding another layer to my understanding of property management. Building the barn itself was an incredible journey. I started with an open cornfield, envisioning it as a horse stable, and I hired the right people to bring that vision to life. Buying the land on a contract posed its own challenges—financing was difficult, and it took perseverance to get everything in place.

Years later, when I considered purchasing a studio, I applied this experience to explore the option of seller financing. Through each of these experiences, I've learned invaluable lessons, especially about real estate, that I'm always eager to share with others.

CHAPTER 7
ARTISTIC AND SPIRITUAL AWAKENING

The Night the Flames Came

October 30, 2016, began like any ordinary night. The Cubs were playing in the World Series - a miracle in itself for this lifelong Chicagoan. My husband and I drifted off to sleep with the faint sound of the game in the background, our three dogs and two cats settled into their usual places around the house. The thought of anything extraordinary happening seemed as distant as the flicker of stars over the Barnegat Bay outside our window.

Then came Halloween morning, around 3:30 a.m. My

husband awoke first, noticing a strange, flickering light outside our bedroom windows. Our room had tall windows that opened up to the bay, and usually, I loved watching the night lights reflected in the water. But this light was different, strange enough to jolt him awake. He nudged me, urgency sharp in his voice. "Get up. The house is on fire."

Groggy and disoriented, I barely registered the words, but he was already on his feet, running downstairs to grab a fire extinguisher. I grabbed my phone, instinctively dialing 911. As I reached the top of the stairs, the flames were already licking up the back of the house. It felt surreal, a scene that should only play out on television, not in the home we'd only begun to settle into. The flames illuminated the windows, casting an eerie glow over our world.

My husband's priority was to get our pets out, starting with the puppy we'd just adopted weeks before. She was crated downstairs near the back door. Miraculously, he opened the crate with one motion, and she shot out toward me, just as I made it to the entryway. I scooped her up, heart pounding, my mind racing through all the "what ifs." How had this even started? Was it a gas leak? A forgotten appliance? But there was no time to answer those questions. The fire was here, and it was consuming everything.

One of our other dogs followed me outside, but one, Maggie, panicked and darted back upstairs. My husband wouldn't leave her behind. He charged up after her, calling her name through the smoke. Even in those few moments, the fire had devoured the oxygen in the room, choking him as he called out to her. Finally, Maggie responded, bolting down the stairs toward the safety of our front yard.

We gathered ourselves in the driveway, three dogs shivering against the October chill, as we scrambled into my husband's car to stay warm. The adrenaline masked the cold, our shock turning every moment into something dreamlike. my husband phoned his son, who lived nearby, barely able to get the words out - "Our house is on fire."

Within minutes, our small community came to life. Our elderly neighbor with his dog, our other neighbors across the street, who welcomed us into their home in our nightclothes, even the police officer who offered to shelter us in his patrol car. We sat there, crushed into the small backseat with three dogs, waiting as firefighters worked on the blaze.

From across the street, I could see flames bursting through the front windows. That was the moment it truly hit me. Up until then, some small part of me hoped they'd put it out, that we'd go back in, damaged but salvageable. But as the flames poured out of those windows, it felt as though our entire life was engulfed, leaving nothing behind.

The firemen worked tirelessly, but it took hours. My best friend flew in the next morning, showing up without question or hesitation. She became our rock through those days, organizing our thoughts and our tasks, a grounding force as we faced the rubble that had been our home. She knew instinctively what I needed even when I didn't, becoming not just a friend but an anchor.

In the days that followed, reality sank in. We moved into what I called our "three-room mansion" - a hotel suite with two bedrooms and a kitchenette where we stayed with our three dogs and our one surviving cat, Jack, whom my husband had miraculously found cowering in the burnt shell of our home. Everything else was gone. I didn't cry for the loss of our belongings - at least, not at first. But one afternoon, as we were walking through a mall to buy essentials, it hit me. Among the lost items was my iittala glassware, a family collection passed down from my mother. The real loss washed over me in that moment, standing there surrounded by the bustle of the mall. I started to cry, only to realize that no tears would bring back those memories. Moving forward was our only option.

Life became a blur of decisions, purchases, and steps toward rebuilding. We still had our work, and my art, something I'd only just rekindled after years. I clung to it, using drawing as a way to process the trauma, creating pieces that captured both the chaos and resilience we were living. In a twist of fate, I turned those drawings into my children's book, *Once Upon a Tile: Suzi's Shoer & her Superpower* inspired by the strange, comforting images I had once seen in the bathroom tiles of our home. In a way, art became a way to rebuild the parts of me the fire had threatened to erase.

Months later, we sat with the insurance adjuster, listing every item lost, from furniture to photo albums. It was exhausting, like replaying the fire a thousand times. But my mentor's words rang in my mind: "Focus on what remains." In a way, that was the ultimate lesson. Even amid loss, we had each other, our dogs, and new opportunities to shape our lives. We found a new home in New Jersey, as well as another in Michigan - a town from my childhood. We would start again with a new chapter.

Halloween will never be the same, always a reminder of the flames that tried to consume more than just our home. But each year, I'm reminded too of what survived, the unbreakable threads of friendship, love, and resilience that no fire could ever destroy.

I had decided put my studio on the market—the building itself—and there was a "For Sale" sign on the front door. Lately, people had been coming up to me with sympathetic faces, asking, "Are you really closing the studio?" as if it's a sad farewell. But I realized I wasn't sad, nor am I sorry. This decision was made with intention, just like the decisions to buy the building and open it. This isn't a failure, and I'm certainly not here grieving. It was simply time to move forward.

I began my journey in the artisan center nearby, with the help and support of my mentor, someone who has been there for me, teaching and guiding me. During a converstions with another artist, I was asked "what's next?" I told him I wasn't sure yet; part of the challenge in deciding to close the studio was not having a clear image of what comes next. But I also knew that I didn't have to have every detail figured out at that moment.

People often want a conclusion they can feel comfortable with, but I've realized I don't have to meet anyone else's expectations or fit into someone else's story. This chapter is mine to write.

My time in pottery hasn't been without challenges. At one point, I dealt with some truly toxic individuals, and it reached a point where I had a physical reaction just being around that environment. I had to push through and I knew it was time to walk away from negativity that drained my energy.

This decision to close the studio aligns with my principles – the Queen Code that I live by. It's about maintaining boundaries, honoring myself, and recognizing when it's time to let go. This choice wasn't made lightly or overnight. But now, But it was clear, it's time to move on.

It's interesting that bookkeeping has been the one constant in my adult life—it's always been there. I know it's challenging for many people, but for me, it just makes sense; numbers come naturally to me. It's almost second nature, allowing me to handle it efficiently and then move on to the next thing, whatever that may be.

Balancing this with my creative work is something I find really fulfilling, but ultimately, numbers just make sense to me.

Laura Muirhead

CHAPTER 8
LEGACY AND LOOKING FORWARD

The gentle hum of the Michigan countryside was both a haven and a distraction. Being here always felt like a gift and a test, each visit a mix of rejuvenation and detours. Back in New Jersey, I felt a steadiness, a mental quiet, but Michigan had a way of pulling me in a hundred directions. And it was here, on a sleepy morning in the middle of a seemingly routine trip, that I had one of those "only in my life" moments.

I'd told myself today was meant to be a rare day off. No studio work, no obligations—just an easy day with a few friends, a few chats, nothing significant. But of course, life had other plans. As I chatted with a friend who ran the store next to mine, Dan took it upon himself to open the studio for just a few minutes. Just long enough, he laughed later, to sell a towel. He held it up triumphantly, a small trophy of his "studio success." We both laughed at the irony, me musing about the randomness of life's little interventions, him amused by his newfound knack for retail.

Our life was built on these kinds of unpredictable moments, the plans that never really went as planned. And for better or worse, I'd learned to let the tide take me where it wanted. Sometimes, that meant wading into complicated family waters.

I received the box on an unassuming afternoon, handed over with a quiet reverence by my son. My mother had sent it along, he explained, but not without a curious twist. The box had come to me from my sister, via my mother, and sent to my son. It was filled with a peculiar collection of our family's past. Inside were photos, faded images of days long past, memories of my childhood and my daughter's baby days, yellowed corners and all.

Seeing those pictures was like opening a lost piece of myself. Each photo held a memory, the delicate snap of a camera capturing not just an image, but a feeling, a time, a version of me that had been left behind. There was a photo of me bringing my daughter home from the hospital, her tiny face nestled against my chest, my hair pulled back in the haphazard way of new mothers.

It was odd to realize these were the very memories my sister had hidden, memories I almost lost forever. A wave of something bitter sweet swept over me; a mixture of disbelief and sadness. I'd lost so many photographs in the fire, years of memories erased by the flames. And yet here, after all these years, was a strange hand-me-down box of my life. I wondered why my mother hadn't handed them over with a simple smile. Instead, she'd chosen this odd, backhanded delivery.

Sometimes, the people closest to us become mysteries. And sometimes, in their own quiet, unassuming ways, they remind us of the preciousness of the past, even the complicated pasts we carry forward.

My connection to stories didn't end at the boundaries of my family. Here in Michigan, I'd found myself drawn to another circle of stories—those of the Oceana County Foundation. A few years ago, my husband and I had set up a fund with the foundation, one designed to support those who needed a nudge forward, people with dreams and skills they couldn't quite put into action alone. There was a particular program we'd supported, "Complete Your Degree," that helped adults finish their education or trade skills. One of our scholarship recipients, a young man, had completed his training as an electrician, and the foundation had asked me to present him with a set of tools to mark his achievement.

I still remember that night. Standing in front of a room full of friends, strangers, and community members, I looked down at the polished metal tools in my hand, ready to hand them over to this man whose story I only barely knew. His face lit up as I placed them in his hands. His pride was unmistakable, the joy in his eyes a mirror of my own, of all of us who'd ever wanted to do something meaningful with our lives.

As he spoke that night, he told us he was the first in his family to complete his education. His words left me nearly speechless; I hadn't known just how much this meant to him, hadn't imagined the ripples this one small gesture would create in his life. I left the dinner that night with a renewed understanding of what it meant to be part of something bigger, of how stories could bring people together and fuel a kind of change that went beyond numbers and donations.

There was one story that stood out even beyond that. The foundation director, had told me about the children of migrant workers who came to this community each season. Families that moved with the crops, who carried everything they owned in suitcases or duffle bags. She'd said that sometimes the kids arrived without blankets, that parents would forget essentials like shoes or bandanas as they packed for yet another move. And so, every year, the foundation collected donations to fill in those small gaps, to make the children's transitions a little softer, their nights a little warmer.

As I heard the directors words, something tugged at my heart. The next time I saw a list of items they needed, I grabbed as much as I could, filling my trunk with blankets, shoes, anything I could manage. It was a small act, really, but I knew, deep down, it was part of something much larger—a ripple effect, a way of passing forward the kindnesses I'd received, the stories I carried within me, and the hope that had been handed down to me by so many others.

Michigan has taught me many things: that life can be unpredictable, that family ties can be both strong and strange, and that stories - our own and others' - carry the power to connect, to heal, and to guide. When I stepped out into the evening air after delivering those tools to a new electrician or handing over blankets for children I'd never meet, I felt as though my life was more woven into theirs, as if each gesture, each act of giving, was one more thread binding us all together.

The stories I'd carried all these years weren't just mine; they were pieces of a larger tapestry, connecting me to the lives I touched, the people I knew, and even the strangers I'd never meet. And somewhere in this blend of laughter, memory, and hope, I felt something larger, a sense of purpose, of belonging, of being exactly where I was meant to be.

My mom lives in town, but it's been a bit challenging reconnecting with her. I went through a period of time when things felt easier between us, but now it's tricky again, perhaps as so much emotion has been reflected on in writing this book.

I do see her differently than I used to, yet there are still moments when I feel as if I'm almost invisible to her. Yet, she'll say wonderful things about me to others, because people will come up to me saying, "Your mom's so proud of you."

She does try to connect in her own way. She visited my studio recently, asking about the Queen Code cards—checking if they'd arrived yet. She knew it's something that's important to me at the moment.

My kids and I have a great relationship. My daughter is 33 now and is so much like me but even stronger, with solid boundaries—she's got a fierce side that I admire. My son, now 30, and I share a silly, easy humor. He and his fiancée are around often, and my husband doesn't quite get our jokes sometimes. It's almost ridiculously silly when we banter, but I love it. My husband has a great sense of humor too, just different. He once said, "What's up with you and your son?" after watching us joke around.

CONCLUSION

The Buffet

Recently, a couple of my friends were chatting about me. (I know this because one of them told me they were.) They were concerned, thinking that I'm overwhelmed because I have too much on my plate.

I listened to their story with interest. When my friend finished, I said,

"You know none of that is true, right?"

The truth is, I wasn't overwhelmed.

The truth is, everything on my plate is there because I chose it.

If I ever felt overwhelmed, I could chose to take something off my plate - temporarily or permanently.

This brings me to wanting to share something with you…

Imagine you pick up a plate at the beginning of a buffet line. You hold your plate, excited as you look over all the choices. But instead of food, laid out in front of you are choices. Choices of life experiences, emotions, relationships, and energies.

Which ones will you place on your plate, and what will you pass on?

Will your plate be balanced?

What do you do if someone tries to add to your plate? To put their choices onto your plate? Or judge what you've put on your plate? Maybe they'd like to take something from your's that you're not willing to give.

I love the saying, "Keep your eyes on your own plate". Would you be willing to say that to someone? Are you able to do that for yourself? To not judge, take away or add to someone else's plate?

Maybe it's time to clear your plate, having enjoyed what has been there, but now you're ready to make room for fresh, new experiences, relationships, and choices.

Here we are, with all these choices in life. With a plate we can pile high! Sometimes it's hard to remember that we are the ones that get to choose what we want. How we feel, what we create in our lives. How will you fill up your plate?

When you have a Queen Code and solid personal policies in place, you hold the power to choose deliberately. Embrace the buffet of life with confidence, knowing you have the wisdom and strength to create a life filled with what truly nourishes you.

Unlimited Possibilities

For my entire life I've been able to attract what I am passionate about or desire…long before I ever heard the words manifest or co-creation. What I have known for most of my life is that there are unlimited possibilities. I remember after graduating from high school (a year early…one of my 'manifestations') questioning what I wanted to do next with my life. I knew that it was all up to me…and I could do anything I chose! It would be up to me to make it happen. I also knew that I most likely wouldn't be a brain surgeon. If I really applied myself I could do it, but it wasn't something that I was inclined to do, or passionate about. The question has always been what do I want to do, not can I do it, or is it possible. A few of the experiences I chose to attract:

- Earning my private pilot license in my twenties
- My first trip to Finland with my grandparents when I was 14
- Moving from the midwest to California at 18
- Opening a bread store
- Building a horse stable from a cornfield up
- There was the time I was fortunate with the lottery
- Reconnecting with and marrying my husband after twenty something years
- When our house burned down, we saw an opportunity to have two homes in different states, and then I opened an art studio

- Publishing a children's book, journals, and co-authoring an international best seller
- Training in LightWeb® and certifying as a LightWeb® Priestess
- Hosting my A Funny Thing Happened On The Way To My Life® podcast
- Creating my signature Queen Code program, helping women to set personal policies and transform their lives.

All of these things didn't just happen. There was a co-creation, meaning that I had to take steps towards what I wanted, moving the desire forward and then universal energy met me in creating the desired results. There have also been times when I realize that things weren't coming together to reach my goal in the timing or way that I had hoped. In those times, I've learned that sometimes a pause can be more valuable than trying to push things through. Sometimes that pause allows for more information to be gathered, for that 'aha' moment to happen, or even for the universe to unfold options that hadn't been on my radar. We create our lives moment by moment day by day. When we choose what we really want and have personal responsibility for taking action to move our desires forward, the universe will meet us in creating magic in our lives!

BUSINESS LESSONS

Nobody starts a business with the intention to fail.

When I decided to create my first business, a bread store, it was with great hope and anticipation. There was a lot to learn. I knew I couldn't do it on my own so I partnered with my best friends and her husband all of us brought unique skills to the tble and it seemed like a winning combination.

Little did we know that the business model we we using was flawed from the start since the franchisor was less than transparent and honest with us.

I still remember my nervousness as I entered the Chicago high rise and went up the elevator to meet our potential landlord. It felt like being in a very adult world that I hadn't experienced before.

We did secure a lease, and a lawyer, and an accountant. We bought all the right equipment and thought we we doing all the right things.

And yet it didn't workout.

It was a devastating time for me. I was blamed for the failure, after all, it was my idea and I was determined to make it happen.

People would tell me that there is something good in everything. It definitely didn't feel that way at the time. Over the years I have come to accept that it was a learning experience, but I am still sad about the loss of my close friendship because of it.

Not long after that I had a deep desire to have my own horse stable. There was a real argument within myself because of my previous business loss. Eventually my passion won.

I bought a 40 acre cornfield and hired a well known company to build my dream. Again, there were lessons learned. Banking and finance lessons, people that took advantage and luckily, people that were honest, loyal friends who contributed their skills and advice.

This business was a much better success than my first one, thank goodness! I'm fortunate to still have strong connections to many of the people I met along the way.

I felt that much of my previous work experience was brought together in running my stable. The pieces just seemed to fit.

In order to focus more of my time on my children, the stable was sold when I divorced

And yet every step I had previously taken added more

tools to my toolbox.

When I reconnected with my current husband, he was already a business owner. The company has been in business since 1929. It was family owned until the last member of that family passed on, leaving no direct heirs to take over. Realizing that if the company folded, he and all the other employees would be out of jobs, my husband made a tough deal to buy the company over 4 years. It was a really hard four years as the contract was set up for him to fail. Regardless, he succeeded by the skin of his teeth in completing the purchase.

By the time I came into the picture he had been running everything himself for several years. We realized that my financial skill set, and professional experiences could compliment his hard working, hands on knowledge and benefit the company. I was brought in as an owner, Vice President and CFO.

The foundation was already in place when I came on board. Over the last 15 years we've navigated ups and downs, and learned to balance our personal relationship with running the business.

It's not easy for a solo business owner to bring in a partner, trust them and accept new ideas. Luckily, over the years, I've worn him down to listen to me more. A lot more!

As I've continued to learn, grow and change my mindset, our company has also grown exponentially. Our sales have doubled with increasing profits. I am happy to say we are having our best year yet. Seeing the results, even my old school husband reluctantly admits that a positive mindset and energy are game changers.

We are grateful to have a hardworking, skilled team of employees that support the work we do, yet acknowledge the responsibility we have to them as owners.

This year we celebrate 95 years in business and hope to leave a long legacy for future generations of our family.

AUTHORS NOTE

I want to leave youwith some thing to think about ...

Even as I finalize writing and editing this book I've been given a lesson that I want to share with you.

Dreams that I didn't know I had came true!

Having my book *A Funny Thing Happened On The Way To My Life* broadcast on a Times Square billboard is something I never imagined. In my whole life I never even thought of being on a billboard in Times Square. And yet there it was ...*there I was* ... in the middle of Times Square, New York City, surrounded by family and friends celebrating exactly that.

In fact, younger me wouldn't have imagined being the author of my own book because I was never meant to be the writer.

So how did it happen? How did such an unexpected and incredible experience come to me?

Being open to allowing your journey to unfold, and to saying yes to things that feel aligned and inspired is the key to magic happening in our lives. When I said yes to finally telling my story, guided and supported by people that felt right to me, trusting them with walking with me, opportunities unfolded.

I am grateful for the opportunities and saying YES to all of them!

I'm grateful that somehow there was always something in me that drove me to do well for *myself*. To have a desire to follow my passions, and yes there have been a few, whether it was horses, flying airplanes, starting and running businesses, art and creativity, or, yes, writing. I have published and illustrated a children's book, a series of three journals and have become an international best selling author. And now the author of my own memoir, that was on a billboard… in Times Square.

Hold on to your dreams, put them out into the universe, and say yes to opportunities that feel aligned. Who knows … may be your undiscovered dreams will come true too!

Stay tuned … there's more to come.

ABOUT THE AUTHOR

Laura Muirhead is an international bestselling author, accomplished artist and the CFO of her family's multimillion-dollar company. She is also the creator of the Queen Code program and the Queen Code Oracle Card Deck, which guide multi-passionate women to find clarity, set boundaries and elevate both life and business, stepping into their full potential. Laura's work bridges creativity and business, demonstrating that success can be achieved on both sides of the spectrum.

Her personal journey is as dynamic as her professional life – she is a licensed pilot, an energy healer and the author of A Funny Thing Happened on the Way to My Life, as well as a beloved children's book and three journals. Laura's life story is one of resilience and reinvention. From navigating the unexpected twists of life to rebuilding after a devastating house fire, she draws inspiration from her experiences to empower others.

Laura enjoys photography and exploring the world. She splits her time between homes in New Jersey and Michigan. Laura cherishes time with her husband, grown children, close friends, two Labrador retrievers and a life filled with creativity and adventure. Learn more about Laura by visiting lauramuirhead.com

To hear more from Laura and her story,
scan the link below:

www.ingramcontent.com/pod-product-compliance
Lightning Source LLC
Chambersburg PA
CBHW020545080526